Moving to America

Janet Maule Swartz

Illustrated by Ana Marie Andronescu

Dominie Press, Inc.

The development of the *Carousel Readers* was supported by the Reading Recovery project at California State University, San Bernardino. All authors' royalties from the sale of the *Carousel Readers* will be used to support various Reading Recovery projects.

Publisher: Raymond Yuen
Illustrator: Ana Marie Andronescu
Cover Designer: Pamela Pettigrew-Norquist

Published by

Dominie Press, Inc.
1949 Kellogg Avenue
Carlsbad, California 92008 USA

ISBN 1-56270-371-4
Printed in Singapore by PH Productions.

4 5 6 7 PH 98 97 96

We are leaving our home
in Scotland.
We are moving to America.

We pack our things
in large wooden boxes.

We get on a big ship
to sail across the ocean.

We eat on the ship.

We sleep on the ship.

We play on the ship.

Finally we come to America.
We are really excited.

We have not seen our family
for a long time.

They recognize us because
David is wearing his kilt.

We are happy to be in America.